EASY
GERMAN
PHRASE BOOK
Over 740 Basic Phrases
for Everyday Use

DOVER PUBLICATIONS, INC.
NEW YORK

Copyright

Copyright © 1957, 1986, 1994 by Dover Publications, Inc.
All rights reserved under Pan American and International Copyright Conventions.

Published in Canada by General Publishing Company, Ltd., 30 Lesmill Road, Don Mills, Toronto, Ontario.
Published in the United Kingdom by Constable and Company, Ltd., 3 The Lanchesters, 162–164 Fulham Palace Road, London W6 9ER.

Bibliographical Note

The material in this book was originally published by Dover in 1957 as part of a manual to accompany a recording entitled *Listen & Learn German*. The English outline was prepared by the editorial staff of Dover Publications, Inc. The German translation and transliteration were prepared by Gustave Mathieu and Guy Stern.

Library of Congress Cataloging-in-Publication Data

Easy German phrase book : over 740 basic phrases for everyday use.
     p.   cm.
    "The material in this book was originally published by Dover in 1957 as part of a manual to accompany a recording entitled Listen & learn German. The English outline was prepared by the editorial staff of Dover Publications, Inc. The German translation and transliteration were prepared by Gustave Mathieu and Guy Stern"—T.p. verso.
    Includes index.
    ISBN 0-486-28084-5 (pbk.)
    1. German language—Conversation and phrase books—English. I. Dover Publications, Inc.
PF3121.E17   1994
438.3'421—dc20   94–12190
                                                CIP

Manufactured in the United States of America
Dover Publications, Inc., 31 East 2nd Street, Mineola, N.Y. 11501

CONTENTS

INTRODUCTION

This book is designed to teach you the basic words, phrases and sentences that you will need for simple everyday communication in Germany, Austria and parts of Switzerland.* It does not attempt to teach you the grammatical structure of German, but instead helps you to express your needs and handle problems encountered while traveling.

The value of the book rests as much on what is omitted as on what is included. An effort has been made to include only those phrases pertinent to the needs of the traveler. You will find the phrase "Can I have some small change" (a frequent need in travel), but do not expect to find a sentence like "This is the pen of my aunt." Furthermore, since the material presented here is not cumulative, as it is in conventional foreign-language courses, you need not start at the beginning. Study whichever phrases will be the most useful to you.

The focus of instruction is on what *you* will say. However, the section entitled "Making Yourself Understood," which contains such vital phrases as "Please speak more slowly" and "Repeat it, please," will aid you in understanding others.

This book is complete in itself and is meant to be used for reference and study. Read it at odd moments and try to learn ten or fifteen phrases a day. Also, be sure to take the manual with you when you go abroad. All that you have learned will be available for reference and review.

The book is designed to help you form additional German sentences from the sentences it provides. You can do this by substituting a new word for a given word in a familiar sentence. In sentences where this is possible, the candidate for substitution appears in brackets, and is sometimes followed by possible alternatives. For example,

I am a [student]
—teacher
—businessman

*Although German vocabulary, pronunciation and grammar will differ somewhat from region to region, you should be understood without difficulty wherever German is spoken. German is also an important second language in many Eastern European countries.

provides three sentences: "I am a student," "I am a teacher" and "I am a businessman."

Another especially helpful feature is the extensive topic and word index beginning on page 60. Notice that each entry in the book is numbered and that the index refers to these numbers. This enables you to locate information you need quickly, without having to search the entire page.

GERMAN PRONUNCIATION

This book uses a phonetic transcription as an aid to correct pronunciation. (See "Scheme of Pronunciation," below.) It usually appears below the German line in the text.

Most German sounds will present no difficulty for speakers of English. Those sounds that have no English equivalent are marked with an arrow in the Scheme of Pronunciation below.

Long and Short Vowels

German has both long and short vowels. As a general rule, vowels are long when followed by a single consonant or by *h*, or when doubled, and short when followed by two or more consonants. (There are a few exceptions among common, one-syllable words such as *von, man* and *mit*, to which the phonetic transcriptions will serve as a guide.)

Note that the difference between a long and short vowel may change the meaning of a German word: *Staat* "state," *Stadt* "town"; *Stil* "style," *still* "quiet"; *Ofen* "stove," *offen* "open."

Voiced and Voiceless Consonants

In German, a consonant is voiceless (pronounced without vibrating the vocal cords) at the end of a word or syllable. (See Scheme of Pronunciation, below.)

SCHEME OF PRONUNCIATION

Letters	Tran-scription	Example	Notes
a	ah	as in father	Short *a* more nearly resembles the *a* in *a*ha.
b	b	as in boy	*b* is pronounced *p* at the end end of a word or syllable.
c	ts OR k	as in ca*ts* OR *k*ite	*c* rarely occurs outside of combinations of consonants, except in words of foreign origin. For the pronunciation of *c* in the combinations *sch*, *ck* and *ch*, see below.
d	d	as in day	*d* is pronounced *t* at the end of a word or syllable.
e	ay (long)	as in gate, but cut short	Pronounce *ay* as a single pure vowel, not a diphthong; do not slide over into an *ee* sound as we do in English.
	e OR eh (short) uh (mute)	as in met	At the end of a word, *e* is a neutral vowel as in buss*e*s.
f	f	as in *f*all	
g	g	as in go	*g* is pronounced *k* at the end of a word or syllable. Final *g* is usually pronounced *ch* (palatal) after *i*. In a few words of French origin, *g* is pronounced as in massa*g*e. *g* is never pronounced as in *g*em.

Letters	Tran-scription	Example	Notes
h	h	as in *h*old	*h* is silent after a vowel.
i	ee (long)	as in f*ee*l, but cut short	Pronounce *ee* as a single pure vowel, not a diphthong; do not slide over into a *y* sound as we do in English.
	i OR ih (short)	as in h*i*t	
j	y	as in *y*es	
k	k	as in *k*ite	
l	l	as in *l*et	Never like the "dark" *l* in coo*l*.
m	m	as in *m*et	
n	n	as in *n*et	
o	o OR oh (long)	as in n*o*tify, but cut short	Pronounce *o* or *oh* as a single pure vowel, not a diphthong; do not slide over into an *oo* sound as we do in English.
	aw (short)	as in l*aw*yer, but cut short	When a short *o* is followed by r, it has been transcribed as o.
p	p	as in *p*et	
qu	kv	as in la*ck v*ariety	
r	r	somewhat like in *r*ed	*r* may either be trilled with the tip of the tongue, as in Spanish or Italian, or produced by vibrating the uvula (the fleshy lobe in the back of the mouth) against the back of the tongue, as in French.
s	s, z OR sh	as in *s*ee, *z*eal OR *sh*ell	Pronounced z at the beginning of a word or between vowels.

Letters	Tran- scription	Example	Notes
			Pronounced *sh* in the combinations *st* and *sp* when they occur at the beginning of a word or syllable. Elsewhere, or when doubled, *s* is pronounced as in *see*.
t	t	as in *t*ake	
u	oo (long)	as in f*oo*d	Pronounce *oo* as a single pure vowel, not a diphthong; do not slide over into a *w* sound as we do in English.
	o͝o (short)	as in f*oo*t	
v	f	as in *f*it	
w	v	as in *v*ase	
x	ks	as in loo*ks*	
y	(varies)		Occurs only in foreign words and is usually pronounced *ü* or as in the foreign language.
z	ts	as in ca*ts*	
ä	ay (long)	as in g*a*te, but cut short	See note on long *e*, above.
	e OR eh (short)	as in m*e*t	
ö	e̅r̅		Do not pronounce the *r* itself. Pronounced like in French sœ*u*r. Round the lips to say *oh*, and without changing the position of the lips, say *ay*.
ü	ew		Like in the French word r*ue*. Round the lips to say *oo*, and without changing the position of the lips, say *ee*.
ch	kh (guttural)	as in Scottish lo*ch*	*ch* is guttural after *a*, *o* and *u*; palatal (see below) elsewhere.

Letters	Tran- scription	Example	Notes
$\overline{\text{sh}}$ (palatal)			You will be understood if you say *sh* as in *sh*ell, or an exaggerated breathy *h* as in *h*uge. Try to pronounce *sh* with the tip of the tongue against the lower gums.
chs	ks	as in loo*ks*	
ch	k	as in ba*ck*	
ng	ng	as in si*ng*er; never as in hu*ng*er	
sch	sh	as in *sh*ell	

Diphthongs

Letters	Tran-scription	Example
ai, ei	$\overline{\text{i}}$	as in *k*ite, but cut short
au	ow	as in *c*ow; never as in low
äu, eu	oy	as in *boy*, but cut short

SOCIAL CONVERSATION

1. Good morning.
Guten Morgen.
GOO-ten MOR-gen.

2. Good evening.
Guten Abend.
GOO-ten AH-bent.

3. Hello.
Guten Tag.
GOO-ten tahk.

4. Goodbye.
Auf Wiedersehen.
owf VEE-der-zay-en.

5. I wish to make an appointment with Mr. Braun.
Ich möchte eine Verabredung mit Herrn Braun treffen.
ish MERSH-tuh I-nuh fehr-AHP-ray-doong mit hehrn brown TREF-fen.

6. May I introduce [Mr., Mrs.] Miss Müller?
Darf ich [Herrn, Frau] Fräulein Müller vorstellen?
dahrf ish [hehrn, frow] FROY-lin MEWL-ler FOR-shtel-len?

7. My wife.
Meine Frau.
MI-nuh frow.

8. My husband.
Mein Mann.
min mahn.

9. My daughter.
Meine Tochter.
MI-nuh TAWKH-ter.

10. My son.
Mein Sohn.
min zohn.

11. My sister.
Meine Schwester.
MI-nuh SHVES-ter.

12. My brother.
Mein Bruder.
min BROO-der.

13. My child.
Mein Kind.
min kint.

14. My friend.
Mein Freund (*masc.*).
min froynt.

15. I am glad to meet you.
Sehr angenehm.
zehr AHN-geh-naym.

16. How are you?
Wie geht es Ihnen?
vee gayt es EE-nen?

17. Fine, thanks, and you?
Gut, danke, und Ihnen?
goot, DAHNG-kuh, oont EE-nen?

18. How are things?
Was gibt's sonst?
vahs gipts zawnst?

19. So, so.
Es geht so.
es gayt zo.

20. All right.
Gut.
goot.

21. How is your family?
Wie geht es Ihrer Familie?
vee gayt es EE-rer fah-MEEL-yuh?

22. Please sit down.
Bitte nehmen Sie Platz.
BIT-tuh NAY-men zee plahts.

23. I had a very nice time.
Es war sehr nett.
es vahr zehr net.

24. Give my regards to your aunt and uncle.
Grüssen Sie Ihre Tante und Ihren Onkel von mir.
GREW-sen zee EE-ruh TAHN-tuh oont EE-ren
AWNG-kel fun meer.

25. Come to see us.
Besuchen Sie uns.
beh-ZOO-khen zee oons.

26. May I call on you again?
Darf ich Sie wieder besuchen?
dahrf ish zee VEE-der beh-ZOO-khen?

27. I like you very much.
Ich habe Sie sehr gern.
ish HAH-buh zee zehr gehrn.

28. Congratulations!
Herzliche Glückwünsche!
HEHRTS-lih-shuh GLEWK-vewn-shuh!

29. Happy Birthday!
Herzlichen Geburtstag!
HEHRTS-lih-shen geh-BOORTS-tahk!

30. Happy New Year!
Glückliches Neujahr!
GLEWK-lih-shes NOY-yahr!

31. Merry Christmas!
Fröhliche Weihnachten!
FRĒR-lih-shuh VĪ-nahkh-ten!

YOURSELF

32. My name is John.
Ich heisse Johann.
ish HĪ-suh YO-hahn.

33. I am an American citizen.
Ich bin Bürger der Vereinigten Staaten.
ish bin BEWR-ger dehr fehr-Ī-nish-ten SHTAH-ten.

34. My mailing address is Hotel Adler, Berlin.
Meine Postadresse ist Hotel Adler, Berlin.
*MĪ-nuh PAWST-ah-dres-suh ist ho-TEL AHT-ler,
behr-LEEN.*

35. I am a [student.]
Ich bin [Student].*
ish bin shtoo-DENT.

36. —— teacher.
Lehrer.*
LAY-rer.

37. —— businessman.
Geschäftsmann.
geh-SHEFTS-mahn.

38. I am a friend of Frank's.
Ich bin ein Freund von Franz.†
ish bin in froynt fun frahnts.

39. I am here on vacation.
Ich mache eine Ferienreise.
ish MAH-khuh Ī-nuh FEHR-yen-ri-zuh.

40. I am here on a business trip.
Ich mache eine Geschäftsreise.
ish MAH-khuh Ī-nuh geh-SHEFTS-ri-zuh.

41. I am traveling to Berlin.
Ich reise nach Berlin.
ish RĪ-zuh nahkh behr-LEEN.

42. I am [hungry] thirsty.
Ich habe [Hunger] Durst.
ish HAH-buh [HOŎNG-er] doŏrst.

---

*The feminine forms of *Student* and *Lehrer* are *Studentin* and *Lehrerin*.
† A woman would say *Ich bin eine Freundin von Franz.*

43. I am in a hurry.
Ich habe es eilig.
ish HAH-buh es Ī-lish.

MAKING YOURSELF UNDERSTOOD

44. Do you speak English?
Sprechen Sie Englisch?
SHPREH-shen zee ENG-lish?

45. Does anyone here speak English?
Spricht hier jemand Englisch?
shprisht heer YAY-mahnt ENG-lish?

46. I speak only English.
Ich spreche nur Englisch.
ish SHPREH-shuh noor ENG-lish.

47. I can read a little German.
Ich kann ein bisschen Deutsch lesen.
ish kahn in BIS-shen doytsh LAY-zen.

48. Please speak more slowly.
Bitte, sprechen Sie langsamer.
BIT-tuh, SHPREH-shen zee LAHNG-zah-mer.

49. I (do not) understand.
Ich verstehe (nicht).
ish fehr-SHTAY-uh (nisht).

50. Do you understand me?
Verstehen Sie mich?
fehr-SHTAY-en zee mish?

51. I (do not) know.
Ich weiss (nicht).
ish vis (nisht).

52. I (do not) think so.
Ich glaube (nicht).
ish GLOW-buh (nisht).

53. Repeat it, please.
Wiederholen Sie es, bitte.
vee-der-HO-len zee es, BIT-tuh.

54. Write it down, please.
Schreiben Sie es, bitte.
SHRĪ-ben zee es, BIT-tuh.

55. What does this word mean?
Was bedeutet dieses Wort?
vahs beh-DOY-tet DEE-zes vort?

56. What is that?
Was ist das?
vahs ist dahs?

57. How do you say "pencil" in German?
Wie sagt man „pencil" auf Deutsch?
vee zahkt mahn "pencil" owf doytsh?

USEFUL WORDS AND EXPRESSIONS

58. Yes.
Ja.
yah.

59. No.
Nein.
nin.

60. Perhaps.
Vielleicht.
fee-LĪSHT.

61. Please.
Bitte.
BIT-tuh.

62. Excuse me.
Entschuldigen Sie.
ent-SHŎŎL-dih-gen zee.

63. Thanks (very much).
Danke (sehr).
DAHNG-kuh (zayr).

64. You are welcome.
Bitte.
BIT-tuh.

65. It is all right.
Es ist gut.
es ist goot.

66. It doesn't matter.
Das macht nichts.
dahs mahkht nishts.

67. That is all.
Das ist alles.
dahs ist AHL-les.

68. Who are you, please?
Wer sind Sie, bitte?
vehr zint zee, BIT-tuh?

69. Who is [that boy]?
Wer is [der Junge] dort?
vehr ist [dehr YŎŎNG-uh] dawrt?

70. —— that girl.
das Mädchen.
dahs MAYD-shen.

71. —— that man.
der Herr.
dehr hehr.

72. —— that woman.
die Dame.
dee DAH-muh.

73. Where is [the men's room]?
Wo ist [die Herrentoilette].
vo ist [dee Hehr-ren-toh-ah-LET-tuh]?

74. —— the ladies' room.
die Damentoilette.
dee DAH-men-toh-ah-LET-tuh.

75. Who?
Wer?
vehr?

76. Why?
Warum?
vah-ROOM?

77. How?
Wie?
vee?

78. What do you wish?
Was wünschen Sie?
vahs VEWN-shen zee?

79. Come here!
Kommen Sie her!
KAWM-men zee HEHR!

80. Come in!
Herein!
hehr-IN!

81. Wait a moment!
Warten Sie einen Augenblick!
VAHR-ten zee I-nen OW-gen-blick!

82. Listen!
Hören Sie zu!
HER-ren zee TSOO!

83. Look out!
Passen Sie auf!
PAHS-sen zee OWF!

DIFFICULTIES AND REPAIRS

84. Can you [help me] tell me?
Können Sie [mir helfen] mir sagen?
KER-nen zee [meer HEL-fen] meer ZAH-gen?

85. I am looking for my friends.
Ich suche meine Freunde.
ish ZOO-khuh MI-nuh FROYN-duh.

86. I cannot find my hotel address.
Ich kann meine Hoteladresse nicht finden.
ish kahn MI-nuh ho-TEL-ah-dres-suh nisht FIN-den.

87. She has lost [her handbag].
Sie hat [ihre Handtasche] verloren.
zee haht [EE-ruh HAHNT-tah-shuh] fehr-LO-ren.

88. —— her wallet.
ihr Portemonnaie.
eer port-mawn-NAY.

89. He forgot [his money].
Er hat [sein Geld] vergessen.
ehr haht [zin gelt] fehr-GES-sen.

90. —— his keys.
seine Schlüssel.
ZI-nuh SHLEWS-sel.

91. My glasses are broken.
Meine Brille ist zerbrochen.
MĪ-nuh BRIL-luh ist tsehr-BRAW-khen.

92. The lost-and-found desk.
Das Fundbüro.
dahs FŎŎNT-bew-ro.

93. The police station.
Das Polizeirevier.
dahs paw-lih-TSĪ-reh-veer.

94. I will call a policemen.
Ich werde einen Polizisten rufen.
ish VEHR-duh Ī-nen paw-lih-TSIH-sten ROO-fen.

95. The American consulate.
Das amerikanische Konsulat.
dahs ah-may-ree-KAH-nish-uh kawn-zoo-LAHT.

CUSTOMS

96. Where is the customs?
Wo is der Zoll?
vo ist dehr tsawl?

97. Here is [my baggage].
Hier ist [mein Gepäck].
heer ist [mīn geh-PEK].

98. —— my passport.
mein Pass.
mīn pahs.

99. —— my identification papers.
mein Ausweis.
mīn OWS-vīs.

100. The bags to the right are mine.
Die Koffer rechts gehören mir.
dee KAWF-fer reshts geh-HĒR-ren meer.

101. I have nothing to declare.
Ich habe nichts zu verzollen.
ish HAH-buh nishts tsoo fehr-TSAWL-len.

102. All this is for my personal use.
All dies ist für meinen persönlichen Gebrauch.
ahl dees ist fewr MĪ-nen pehr-ZERN-lish-en geh-BROWKH.

103. Must I open everything?
Muss ich alles öffnen?
moos ish AHL-les ERF-nen?

104. I cannot open the trunk.
Ich kann den Koffer nicht öffnen.
ish kahn dayn KAWF-fer nisht ERF-nen.

105. There is nothing here but clothing.
Es sind nur Kleidungsstücke darin.
es zint noor KLI-doongs-shtew-kuh dah-RIN.

106. These are gifts.
Dies sind Geschenke.
dees zint geh-SHENG-kuh.

107. Are these things dutiable?
Sind diese Sachen zollpflichtig?
zint DEE-zuh ZAH-khen TSAWL-pflish-tish?

108. How much must I pay?
Wieviel muss ich bezahlen?
VEE-feel moos ish beh-TSAH-len?

109. This is all I have.
Dies ist alles, was ich habe.
dees ist AHL-les, vahs ish HAH-buh.

110. Have you finished?
Sind Sie fertig?
zint zee FEHR-tish?

BAGGAGE

111. Where can I check my baggage through to Berlin?
Wo kann ich mein Gepäck nach Berlin aufgeben?
vo kahn ish min geh-PEK nahkh behr-LEEN OWF-gay-ben?

112. The baggage room.
Der Gepäckraum.
dehr geh-PEK-rowm.

113. The baggage check.
Der Gepäckschein.
dehr geh-PEK-shin.

114. I want to leave these packages for a while.
Ich will diese Pakete eine Zeitlang hier lassen.
*ish vil DEE-zuh pah-KAY-tuh Ī-nuh TSĪT-lahng
heer LAHS-sen.*

115. Handle this very carefully!
Fassen Sie dies sehr vorsichtig an!
FAHS-sen zee dees zehr FOR-sish-tish AHN!

TRAVEL: GENERAL EXPRESSIONS

116. I want to go [to the airline office].
Ich möchte [zum Büro der Fluglinie] gehen.
*ish MERSH-tuh [tsoom BEW-ro dehr FLOOK-leen-
yuh] GAY-en.*

117. —— to the travel agent's office.
zum Reisebüro.
tsoom RĪ-zuh-bew-ro.

118. —— to the tourist information office.
zum Auskunftsbüro.
tsoom OWS-koonfts-bew-ro.

119. —— to the hotel information office.
zum Zimmernachweis.
tsoom TSIM-mer-nahkh-vīs.

120. How long does the trip to Vienna take?
Wie lange dauert die Fahrt nach Wien?
vee LAHNG-uh DOW-ert dee fahrt nahkh veen?

121. When do we arrive in Munich?
Wann kommen wir in München an?
vahn KAWM-men veer in MEWN-shen AHN?

122. Is this the direct way to Zurich?
Ist dies der direkte Weg nach Zürich?
ist dees dehr dee-REK-tuh vayk nahkh TSEW-rish?

123. Please show me the way [to the business section].
.Bitte zeigen Sie mir den Weg [zum Geschäftsviertel].
BIT-tuh TSĪ-gen zee meer dayn vayk [tsoom geh-SHEFTS-fihr-tel].

124. —— to the residential section.
zum Wohnviertel.
tsoom VOHN-feer-tel.

125. —— to the shopping section.
zum Einkaufszentrum.
tsoom ĪN-kowfs-tsen-troom.

126. —— to the city.
zu der Stadt.
tsoo dehr shtaht.

127. —— to the village.
zu dem Dorf.
tsoo daym dorf.

128. Do I turn [to the north]?
Muss ich [nach Norden] abbiegen?
moos ish [nahkh NOR-den] AHP-bee-gen?

129. —— to the south.
nach Süden.
nahkh ZEW-den.

130. —— to the east.
nach Osten.
nahkh AWS-ten.

131. —— to the west.
nach Westen.
nahkh VES-ten.

132. —— to the right.
nach rechts.
nahkh reshts.

133. —— to the left.
nach links.
nahkh links.

134. —— at the traffic light.
bei der Verkehrsampel.
bī dehr fehr-KAYRS-ahm-pel.

135. Where is it?
Wo ist es?
vo ist es?

136. Should I go [this way]?
Soll ich [dieser Strasse] folgen?
zawl ish [DEE-zer SHTRAH-suh] FAWL-gen?

137. —— **that way.**
jener Strasse.
YAY-ner SHTRAH-suh.

138. **Is it [on this side of the street]?**
Ist es [auf dieser Seite der Strasse]?
ist es [owf DEE-zer ZĪ-tuh dehr SHTRAH-suh]?

139. —— **on the other side of the street.**
auf der anderen Seite der Strasse.
owf dehr AHN-deh-ren ZĪ-tuh dehr SHTRAH- suh?

140. —— **across the street.**
gegenüber.
gay-gen-EW-ber.

141. —— **at the corner.**
an der Ecke.
ahn der EK-kuh.

142. —— **in the middle.**
in der Mitte.
in dehr MIT-tuh.

143. —— **straight ahead.**
geradeaus.
geh-RAH-duh-ows.

144. —— **in front of the monument.**
vor dem Denkmal.
for daym DENK-mahl.

145. —— **behind the building.**
hinter dem Gebäude.
HIN-ter daym geh-BOY-duh.

146. **Forward.**
Vorwärts.
FOR-vehrts.

147. **Back.**
Zurück.
tsoo-REWK.

148. **How far is it?**
Wie weit ist es?
vee vit ist es?

149. **What street is this?**
Welche Strasse ist dies?
VEL-shuh SHTRAH-suh ist dees?

TICKETS

150. **Where is the ticket office?**
Wo ist der Fahrkartenschalter?
vo ist dehr FAHR-kahr-ten-shahl-ter?

151. How much is a round-trip ticket to Hamburg?
Wieviel kostet eine Fahrkarte nach Hamburg
hin-und-zurück?
VEE-feel KAW-stet Ĭ-nuh FAHR-kahr-tuh nahkh
HAHM-boorg hin-oont-tsoo-REWK?

152. A one-way ticket.
Eine einfache Fahrkarte.
Ĭ-nuh ĬN-fah-khuh FAHR-kahr-tuh.

153. First class.
Erste Klasse.
EHR-stuh KLAHS-suh.

154. Second class.
Zweite Klasse.
TSVĬ-tuh KLAHS-suh.

155. Local train.
Personenzug.
pehr-ƵOH-nen-tsook.

156. Express train.
Schnellzug.
SHNEL-tsook.

157. A reserved seat.
Eine Platzkarte.
Ĭ-nuh PLAHTS-kahr-tuh.

158. The waiting room.
Der Warteraum.
dehr VAHR-tuh-rowm.

159. Can I stop at Frankfurt on the way?
Kann ich die Fahrt in Frankfurt unterbrechen?
kahn ish dee fahrt in FRAHNK-foort oon-ter-BREH-
shen?

BOAT

160. When must I go on board?
Wann muss ich an Bord gehen?
vahn moos ish ahn bort GAY-en?

161. Bon voyage!
Gute Reise!
GOO-tuh RĬ-zuh!

162. Where is [the purser]?
Wo ist [der Zahlmeister]?
vo ist [dehr TSAHL-mĭ-ster]?

163. —— the captain.
der Kapitän.
dehr kah-pee-TAYN.

164. The deck.
Das Deck.
dahs dek.

165. The cabin.
Die Kabine.
dee kah-BEE-muh.

166. I am seasick.
Ich bin seekrank.
ish bin ƵAY-krahnk.

AIRPLANE

167. Is there bus service to the airport?
Gibt es einen Zubringerdienst zum Flughafen?
gipt es Ĭ-nen TSOO-bring-er-deenst tsoom FLOOK-hah-fen?

168. At what time will they pick me up?
Um wieviel Uhr wird man mich abholen?
ŏom VEE-feel oor veert mahn mish̄ AHP-ho-len?

169. Is flight twenty-three on time?
Kommt Flug dreiundzwanzig pünktlich an?
kawmt flook DRĬ-ŏont-TSVAHN-tsish̄ PEWNKT-lish̄ AHN?

170. How many kilos may I take?
Wieviel Kilo darf ich mitnehmen?
VEE-feel KEE-lo dahrf ish̄ MIT-nay-men?

171. How much per kilo for excess?
Wieviel kostet Übergewicht pro Kilo?
VEE-feel KAW-stet EW-ber-geh-visht pro KEE-lo?

TRAIN

172. Where is the railroad station?
Wo ist der Bahnhof?
vo ist dehr BAHN-hohf?

173. When does the boat-train for Bremerhaven leave?
Wann geht der Verbindungszug zum Schiff nach Bremerhaven?
vahn gayt der fehr-BIN-dŏongs-tsook tsŏom shif nahkh bray-mer-HAH-fen?

174. From what track does the train leave?
Von welchem Bahnsteig fährt der Zug ab?
fun VEL-shem BAHN-shtĭk fehrt dehr tsook AHP?

175. Please open the window.
Bitte, öffnen Sie das Fenster.
BIT-tuh, ÉRF-nen zee dahs FEN-ster.

176. Close the window.
Schliessen Sie das Fenster!
SHLEES-sen zee dahs FEN-ster!

177. Where is [the diner]?
Wo ist [der Speisewagen]?
vo ist [dehr SHPĪ-zuh-vah-gen]?

178. —— the first-class sleeper.
der Schlafwagen.
dehr SHLAHF-vah-gen.

179. —— the second-class sleeper.
der Liegewagen.
dehr LEE-guh-vah-gen.

180. —— the smoking car.
das Raucherabteil.
dahs ROW-kher-ahp-tīl.

181. May I smoke?
Darf ich rauchen?
dahrf ĭsh ROW-khen?

BUS AND STREETCAR

182. What streetcar goes to Augusta Anlage?
Welche Strassenbahn fährt nach der Augusta Anlage?
VEL-shuh SHTRAH-sen-bahn fehrt nahkh dehr ow-GŎOS-tah AHN-lah-guh?

183. The bus stop.
Die Omnibus-Haltestelle.
dee AWM-nih-boos-hahl-tuh-shtel-luh.

184. A transfer.
Eine Umsteigekarte.
Ī-nuh ŎOM-shtī-guh-KAHR-tuh.

185. Where do I get the subway for Chestnut Avenue?
Wo finde ich die Untergrundbahn zur Kastanien-allee?
vo FIN-duh ĭsh dee ŎON-ter-groont-bahn tsoor kah-STAHN-yen-ahl-LAY?

186. Do you go near Bismarck Square?
Fahren Sie in die Nähe des Bismarckplatzes?
FAH-ren zee in dee NAY-uh des BIS-mahrk-PLAHT-tses?

187. Do I have to change?
Muss ich umsteigen?
moos ĭsh ŎOM-shtī-gen?

188. Driver, please tell me where to get off.
Fahrer, bitte sagen Sie mir, wo ich aussteigen muss.
FAH-rer, BIT-tuh ZAH-gen zee meer, vo ish OWS-shti-gen moos.

189. The next stop, please.
Die nächste Haltestelle, bitte.
dee NAYK-stuh HAHL-tuh-shtel-luh, BIT-tuh.

TAXI

190. Please call a taxi for me.
Bitte, rufen Sie mir ein Taxi.
BIT-tuh, ROO-fen zee meer in TAHK-see.

191. Are you free?
Sind Sie frei?
zint zee fri?

192. What do you charge [per hour] per kilometer?
Was berechnen Sie [pro Stunde] pro Kilometer?
vahs beh-RESH-nen zee [pro SHTOON-duh] pro kil-o-MAY-ter?

193. Stop here.
Halten Sie hier!
HAHL-ten zee HEER!

194. Wait for me.
Warten Sie auf mich!
VAHR-ten zee owf mish!

AUTOMOBILE TRAVEL

195. Where can I rent a car?
Wo kann ich ein Auto mieten?
vo kahn ish in OW-toh MEE-ten?

196. I have an international driver's license.
Ich habe einen internationalen Führerschein.
ish HAH-buh I-nen in-tehr-nahts-yo-NAH-len FEW-rehr-shin.

197. A gas station.
Eine Tankstelle.
Ī-nuh TAHNK-shtel-luh.

198. A garage.
Eine Garage.
Ī-nuh gah-RAH-zhuh.

199. A mechanic.
Ein Mechaniker.
īn meh-SHAH-nih-ker.

200. Is the road [good] bad?
Ist die Strasse [gut] schlecht?
ist dee SHTRAH-suh [goot] shlesht?

201. Where does that road go?
Wohin führt die Strasse dort?
vo-HIN fewrt dee SHTRAH-suh dort?

202. What town is this?
Wie heisst diese Stadt?
vee hīst DEE-zuh shtaht?

203. The next city.
Die nächste Stadt.
dee NAYK-stuh shtaht.

204. Can you show me on the map?
Können Sie es mir auf der Karte zeigen?
KĒR-nen zee es meer owf dehr KAHR-tuh TSĪ-gen?

205. How much is gas a liter?
Wieviel kostet ein Liter Benzin?
VEE-feel KAW-stet īn LEE-ter ben-TSEEN?

206. The tank is [empty] full.
Der Tank ist [leer] voll.
dehr tahnk ist [layr] fawl.

207. Give me forty liters.
Geben Sie mir vierzig Liter!
GAY-ben zee meer FEER-tsish LEE-ter!

208. Please [check] change the oil.
Bitte [kontrollieren] wechseln Sie das Öl!
BIT-tuh [kawn-trawl-LEE-ren] VEK-seln zee dahs ērl!

209. Please put water in the battery.
Füllen Sie bitte die Batterie mit Wasser auf!
*FEWL-len zee BIT-tuh dee baht-teh-REE mit
VAHS-ser OWF!*

210. Will you lubricate the car, please?
Schmieren Sie bitte das Auto!
SHMEE-ren zee BIT-tuh dahs OW-toh!

211. Adjust the brakes.
Stellen Sie die Bremsen nach!
SHTEL-len zee dee BREM-sen nahkh!

212. Will you please check the air?
Bitte, prüfen Sie die Luft!
BIT-tuh, PREW-fen zee dee looft!

213. Can you fix the flat tire?
Können Sie den beschädigten Reifen reparieren?
KERN-nen zee dayn beh-SHAY-dish-ten RĪ-fen reh-pah-REE-ren?

214. The engine overheats.
Der Motor wird zu heiss.
dehr mo-TOR veert tsoo hīs.

215. The motor [misses] stalls.
Der Motor [stottert] bleibt stehen.
dehr mo-TOR [STAW-tehrt] blīpt SHTAY-en.

216. May I park here for a while?
Kann ich hier eine Zeitlang parken?
kahn ish heer Ī-nuh TSĪT-lahng PAHR-ken?

HOTEL

217. I am looking for [a good hotel].
Ich suche [ein gutes Hotel].
ish ZOO-khuh [īn GOO-tes ho-TEL].

218. —— an inexpensive hotel.
ein billiges Hotel.
īn BIL-lig-es ho-TEL.

219. —— a boarding house.
eine Pension.
Ī-nuh pen-SYOHN.

220. —— a furnished apartment.
eine möblierte Wohnung.
Ī-nuh mer-BLEER-tuh VO-noong.

221. I (do not) want to be in the center of town.
Ich möchte (nicht) im Zentrum der Stadt sein.
*ish MERSH-tuh (nisht) im TSEN-troom dehr
shtaht zin.*

222. Where it is quiet.
Wo es ruhig ist.
vo es ROO-ish ist.

223. I have a reservation for today.
Ich habe eine Vorbestellung für heute.
*ish HAH-buh I-nuh FOR-beh-shtel-loong fewr HOY-
tuh.*

224. Is there a vacancy?
Ist noch etwas frei?
ist nawkh ET-vahs fri?

225. Do you have a [room]?
Haben Sie [ein Zimmer]?
HAH-ben zee [in TSIM-mer]?

226. —— a single room.
ein Einzelzimmer.
in IN-tsel-tsim-mer.

227. —— a double room.
ein Doppelzimmer.
in DAWP-pel-tsim-mer.

228. —— an air-conditioned room.
ein Zimmer mit Kühlanlage.
in TSIM-mer mit KEWL-ahn-lah-guh.

229. I want a room [with a double bed].
Ich möchte ein Zimmer [mit einem Doppelbett].
*ish MERSH-tuh in TSIM-mer [mit I-nem DAWP-
pel-bet].*

230. —— with twin beds.
mit zwei Einzelbetten.
mit tsvi IN-tsel-bet-ten.

231. —— with a bath.
mit Bad.
mit baht.

232. I want a room [without meals].
Ich möchte ein Zimmer [ohne Mahlzeiten].
*ish MERSH-tuh in TSIM-mer [OH-nuh MAHL-
tsi-ten].*

233. —— for tonight.
für heute Nacht.
fewr HOY-tuh nahkht.

234. —— for several days.
für mehrere Tage.
fewr MAY-reh-ruh TAH-guh.

235. —— **for two persons.**
    für zwei Personen.
    fewr tsvī pehr-ZO-nen.

236. I should like to see the room.
    Ich möchte das Zimmer gern sehen.
    ish MERSH-tuh dahs TSIM-mer gehrn ZAY-en.

237. Is it [upstairs] downstairs?
    Ist es [oben] unten?
    ist es [O-ben] ŎŎN-ten?

238. Room service, please.
    Zimmerbedienung, bitte.
    TSIM-mer-beh-DEE-noong, BIT-tuh.

239. Please send [a porter] to my room.
    Bitte schicken Sie [den Hausdiener] auf mein
      Zimmer.
    BIT-tuh SHIK-ken zee [dayn HOWS-dee-ner] owf
    mīn TSIM-mer.

240. a chambermaid.
    ein Zimmermädchen.
    īn TSIM-mer-mayd-shen.

241. a bellhop.
    ein Hotelpage.
    īn ho-TEL-pah-zhuh.

242. Please wake me at nine-fifteen.
    Bitte wecken Sie mich um neun Uhr fünfzehn.
    BIT-tuh VEK-ken zee mish ōom noyn oor FEWNF-tsayn.

243. I should like to have breakfast in my room.
    Ich möchte auf meinem Zimmer frühstücken.
    ish MERSH-tuh owf MĪ-nem TSIM-mer FREW-shtewk-ken.

244. Who is it?
    Wer ist es?
    vehr ist es?

245. Come back a little later.
    Kommen Sie ein wenig später.
    KAWM-men zee īn VAY-nish SHPAY-ter.

246. Bring me [a blanket].
Bringen Sie mir [eine Decke].
BRING-en zee meer [Ī-nuh DEK-kuh].

247. —— a pillow.
ein Kissen.
in KIS-sen.

248. —— a pillowcase.
einen Kissenbezug.
Ī-nen KIS-sen-beh-tsook.

249. —— sheets.
Laken.
LAH-ken.

250. —— hangers.
Kleiderbügel.
KLĪ-der-BEW-gel.

251. —— soap.
Seife.
ZĪ-fuh.

252. —— towels.
Handtücher.
HAHNT-tew-sher.

253. —— a bath mat.
einen Badeteppich.
Ī-nen BAH-duh-tep-pish.

254. —— toilet paper.
Toilettenpapier.
Toh-ah-LET-ten-pah-peer.

255. I would like to speak to the manager.
Ich möchte mit dem Hoteldirektor sprechen.
ish MERSH-tuh mit daym ho-TEL-dee-rek-tor SHPREH-shen.

256. My room key.
Mein Zimmerschlüssel.
min TSIM-mer-shlews-sel.

257. Have I any letters or messages?
Sind Briefe oder Bestellungen für mich da?
zint BREE-fuh O-der beh-SHTEL-loong-en fewr mish dah?

258. What is my room number?
Was ist meine Zimmernummer?
vahs ist MĪ-nuh TSIM-mer-noom-mer?

259. I am leaving at two o'clock in the afternoon.
Ich fahre um vierzehn Uhr ab.
ish FAH-ruh oom FEER-tsayn oor AHP.

260. Please make out my bill as soon as possible.
Bitte machen Sie meine Rechnung fertig, so bald
   wie möglich.

*BIT-tuh MAH-khen zee MĪ-nuh REŜH-noong
FEHR-tiŝh, zo bahlt vee MĒRG-liŝh.*

261. Are room service and tax included?
Sind Bedienung und Steuer einbegriffen?

zint beh-DEE-noong oont SHTOY-er ĪN-beh-grif-fen?

262. Please forward my mail to this address:
Bitte schicken Sie meine Post an diese Adresse
   nach:

*BĪT-tuh SHIK-ken zee MĪ-nuh pawst ahn DEE-zuh
ah-DRES-suh nahkh:*

AT THE CAFÉ

263. Bartender, I would like [a drink].
Barkellner, ich möchte [ein Getränk].

BAHR-kel-ner, iŝh MĒRŜH-tuh [in geh-TRENK].

264. —— a bottle of mineral water.
eine Flasche Mineralwasser.

Ī-nuh FLAH-shuh mee-neh-RAHL-vahs-ser.

265. —— a glass of sherry.
ein Glas Sherry.

in glahs "sherry."

266. —— [light] dark beer.
[helles] dunkles Bier.

[HEL-les] DOONK-les beer.

267. —— whiskey and soda.
Whisky mit Selter.

VIS-kee mit ZEL-ter.

268. —— brandy.
Schnapps.

shnahps.

269. —— white wine.
Weisswein.

VĪS-vīn.

270. —— red wine.
Rotwein.

ROHT-vīn.

271. —— champagne.
Champagner.

shahm-PAHN-yer.

272. Let's have another round.
Noch eine Runde.

nawhk Ī-nuh RŌON-duh.

273. Cheers!
Prosit!
PRO-zit!

274. To your health!
Zum Wohl!
tsoom vohl!

AT THE RESTAURANT

275. Can you recommend a good restaurant [for dinner]?
Können Sie ein gutes Restaurant [fürs Abend-essen] empfehlen?
KERN-nen zee īn GOO-tes res-toh-RAHNG [fewrs AH-bent-es-sen] emp-FAY-len?

276. —— for breakfast.
fürs Frühstück.
fewrs FREW-shtewk.

277. —— for lunch.
fürs Mittagessen.
fewrs MIT-tahk-es-sen.

278. I want only a sandwich.
Ich möchte nur ein belegtes Brot essen.
ish MERSH-tuh noor īn beh-LAYK-tes broht ES-sen.

279. At what time is supper served?
Wann wird das Abendbrot serviert?
vahn veert dahs AH-bent-broht sehr-VEERT?

280. Are you [my waiter]?
Sind Sie [mein Kellner]?
zint zee [mīn KEL-ner]?

281. —— my waitress.
meine Kellnerin.
mī-nuh KEL-ner-in.

282. —— the headwaiter.
der Oberkellner.
dehr O-ber-kel-ner.

283. Waiter!
Herr Ober!
hehr O-ber!

284. Waitress!
Fräulein!
FROY-līn!

285. Give me a table near the window, please.
Geben Sie mir bitte einen Tisch in der Nähe des Fensters.
GAY-ben zee meer BIT-tuh Ī-nen tish in dehr NAY-uh des FEN-sters.

286. We want to dine à la carte.
Wir wollen à la carte speisen.
veer VAWL-len "à la carte" SHPĪ-zen.

287. We want to dine table d'hôte.
Wir wollen das Menü essen.
veer VAWL-len dahs meh-NEW ES-sen.

288. Bring me [the menu].
Bringen Sie mir [die Speisekarte].
BRING-en zee meer [dee SHPĪ-zuh-kahr-tuh].

289. —— the wine list.
die Weinkarte.
dee VĪN-kahr-tuh.

290. —— a napkin.
eine Serviette.
Ī-nuh zehrv-YET-tuh.

291. —— a fork.
eine Gabel.
Ī-nuh GAH-bel.

292. —— a knife.
ein Messer.
īn MES-ser.

293. —— a plate.
einen Teller.
Ī-nen TEL-ler.

294. —— a teaspoon.
einen Teelöffel.
Ī-nen TAY-ler-fel.

295. —— a soup spoon.
einen Suppenlöffel.
Ī-nen ZOOP-pen-lerf-fel.

296. I would like something [plain].
Ich möchte etwas [Einfaches] essen.
ish MERSH-tuh ET-vahs [ĪN-fah-khes] ES-sen.

297. —— not too spicy.
nicht zu Scharfes.
nisht tsoo SHAHRF-es.

298. —— not too sweet.
nicht zu Süsses.
nisht tsoo ZEWS-ses.

299. —— without fat.
Fettfreies.
FET-fri-es.

300. —— cooked.
Gekochtes.
geh-KAWKH-tes.

301. —— fried.
Gebratenes.
geh-BRAH-teh-nes.

302. I like the meat [rare].
Ich möchte das Fleisch [rosa].
ish MERSH-tuh dahs flīsh RO-zah.

303. ——medium.
    halb durchgebraten.
    hahlp DOORSH-geh-brah-ten.

304. —— well done.
    gut durchgebraten.
    goot DOORSH-geh-brah-ten.

305. Enjoy your meal!
    Guten Appetit!
    GOO-ten ahp-peh-TEET!

306. A little more.
    Ein bisschen mehr.
    in BIS-shen mehr.

307. Enough.
    Genug.
    geh-NOOK.

308. Too much.
    Zu viel.
    tsoo feel.

309. I did not order this.
    Ich habe dies nicht bestellt.
    ish HAH-buh dees nisht beh-SHTELT.

310. Take it away, please.
    Nehmen Sie es fort, bitte.
    NAY-men zee es fort, BIT-tuh.

311. May I change this for a salad?
    Können Sie stattdessen einen Salat bringen?
    KER-nen zee shtaht-DES-sen I-nen zah-LAHT
    BRING-en?

312. The check, please.
    Die Rechnung, bitte.
    dee RESH-noong, BIT-tuh.

313. Is the tip included?
    Ist die Bedienung einbegriffen?
    ist dee beh-DEE-noong IN-beh-grif-fen?

314. There is a mistake in the bill.
    Es ist ein Fehler in der Rechnung.
    es ist in FAY-ler in dehr RESH-noong.

315. What are these charges for?
    Wofür ist dies berechnet?
    VO-fewr ist dees beh-RESH-net?

316. Keep the change.
    Behalten Sie den Rest.
    beh-HAHL-ten zee dayn rest.

317. The food and service were excellent.
Das Essen und die Bedienung waren ausgezeichnet.
dahs ES-sen oont dee beh-DEE-noong VAH-ren
OWS-geh-tsish-net.

FOOD LIST

318. Please bring me some water.
Bitte, bringen Sie mir Wasser.
BIT-tuh BRING-en zee meer VAHS-ser.

319. With ice.
Mit Eis.
mit is.

320. Bread.
Brot.
broht.

321. Butter.
Butter.
BOOT-ter.

322. Sugar.
Zucker.
TSOOK-ker.

323. Salt.
Salz.
zahlts.

324. Pepper.
Pfeffer.
PFEF-fer.

325. Oil.
Öl.
erl.

326. Vinegar.
Essig.
ES-sish.

327. Mustard.
Senf.
zenf.

328. Gravy.
Sosse.
ZOH-suh.

BREAKFAST FOODS

329. May I have some [fruit juice]?
Kann ich etwas [Fruchtsaft] haben?
kahn ish ET-vahs [FROOKHT-zahft] HAH-ben?

330. —— orange juice.
Apfelsinensaft.
ahp-fel-ZEE-nen-zahft.

331. —— tomato juice.
Tomatensaft.
taw-MAH-ten-zahft.

332. —— stewed prunes.
gekochte Dörrzwetschen.
geh-KAWKH-tuh DERR-tsvet-shen.

333. —— **oatmeal.**
Haferschleim.
HAH-fer-shlīm.

334. —— **toast and jam.**
Toast und Marmelade.
tohst ŏont mahr-meh-LAH-duh.

335. —— **rolls.**
Brötchen.
BRĒRT-shen.

336. —— **an omelet.**
ein Omelett.
īn awm-LET.

337. —— **soft-boiled eggs.**
weich gekochte Eier.
vīsh geh-KAWKH-tuh Ī-er.

338. —— **four-minute eggs.**
gekochte Eier.   Vier Minuten.
geh-KAWKH-tuh Ī-er.   feer mih-NOO-ten.

339. —— **hard-boiled eggs.**
harte Eier.
HAHR-tuh Ī-er.

340. —— **scrambled eggs.**
Rühreier.
REWR-ī-er.

341. —— **fried eggs.**
Spiegeleier.
SHPEE-gel-ī-er.

342. —— **ham and eggs.**
Eier mit Schinken.
Ī-er mit SHINK-en.

SOUPS AND ENTRÉES

343. I want some [chicken soup].
Ich möchte [Hühnersuppe].
ish MĒRSH-tuh [HEW-ner-zŏop-puh].

344. —— **vegetable soup.**
Gemüsesuppe.
geh-MEW-zuh-zŏop-puh.

345. —— **beef.**
Rindfleisch.
RINT-flīsh.

346. —— **roast beef.**
Roastbeef.
"roast beef."

347. —— **roast chicken.**
Brathuhn.
BRAHT-hoon.

348. —— **duck.**
Ente.
EN-tuh.

349. —— **fish.**
Fisch.
fish.

350. —— **goose.**
Gans.
gahns.

351. —— **lamb.**
Lamm.
lahm.

352. —— **liver.**
Leber.
LAY-ber.

353. —— **lobster.**
Hummer.
HŎŎM-mer.

354. —— **oysters.**
Austern.
OW-stern.

355. —— **pork.**
Schwein.
shvīn.

356. —— **sardines.**
Sardinen.
zahr-DEE-nen.

357. —— **sausage.**
Wurst.
voorst.

358. —— **shrimps.**
Krabben.
KRAHB-ben.

359. —— **steak.**
Steak.
"steak."

360. —— **veal.**
Kalb.
kahlp.

VEGETABLES AND SALAD

361. I want some [asparagus].
Ich möchte [Spargel].
ish MERSH-tuh [SHPAHR-gel].

362. —— beans.
Bohnen.
BOH-nen.

363. —— cabbage.
Kohl.
kohl.

364. —— carrots.
Karotten.
kah-RAWT-ten.

365. —— cauliflower.
Blumenkohl.
BLOO-men-kohl

366. —— cucumbers.
Gurken.
GOOR-ken.

367. —— lettuce.
Kopfsalat.
KAWPF-zah-laht.

368. —— mushrooms.
Pilze.
PIL-tsuh.

369. —— onions.
Zwiebeln.
TSVEE-beln.

370. —— peas.
Erbsen.
EHRP-sen.

371. —— peppers.
Pfefferschoten.
PFEF-fer-SHOH-ten.

372. —— boiled potatoes.
Salzkartoffeln.
ZAHLTS-kahr-tawf-feln.

373. —— mashed potatoes.
Kartoffelpüree.
kahr-TAWF-fel-pew-ray.

374. —— fried potatoes.
Bratkartoffeln.
BRAHT-kahr-tawf-feln.

375. —— rice.
Reis.
rīs.

376. —— spinach.
Spinat.
shpin-AHT.

377. —— tomatoes.
Tomaten.
toh-MAH-ten.

FRUITS

378. Do you have [cherries]?
Haben Sie [Kirschen]?
HAH-ben zee [KEER-shen]?

379. —— an apple.
einen Apfel.
Ī-nen AHP-fel.

380. —— a grapefruit.
eine Pampelmuse.
Ī-nuh pahm-pel-MOO-zuh.

381. —— grapes.
Trauben.
TROW-ben.

382. —— melon.
eine Melone.
Ī-nuh meh-LO-nuh.

383. —— an orange.
eine Apfelsine.
Ī-nuh ahp-fel-ZEE-nuh.

384. —— a peach.
einen Pfirsich.
Ī-nen PFEER-zish.

385. —— raspberries.
Himbeeren.
HIM-bay-ren.

386. —— strawberries.
Erdbeeren.
EHRT-bay-ren.

BEVERAGES

387. A cup of black coffee.
Eine Tasse schwarzen Kaffee.
Ī-nuh TAHS-suh SHVAHR-tsen kahf-FAY.

388. Coffee with cream.
Kaffee mit Sahne.
kah-FAY mit ZAH-nuh.

389. A glass of milk.
Ein Glas Milch.
in glahs milsh.

390. Tea with lemon.
Tee mit Zitrone.
tay mit tsih-TRO-nuh.

391. Lemonade.
Limonade.
lee-maw-NAH-duh.

392. Soft drinks.
Alkoholfreie Getränke.
AHL-ko-hohl-frī-uh geh-TRENG-kuh.

DESSERTS

393. I should like [some cake].
Ich möchte [ein Stück Kuchen].
ish MERSH-tuh [in shtewk KOO-khen].

394. —— **a piece of pie.**
ein Stück Torte.
īn shtewk TOR-tuh.

395. —— **cheese.**
Käse.
KAY-zuh.

396. —— **cookies.**
Kekse.
KEK-suh.

397. —— **chocolate ice cream.**
Schokoladeneis.
shaw-kaw-LAH-den-īs.

398. —— **vanilla ice cream.**
Vanilleeis.
vah-NIL-luh-īs.

CONVERSATION AT THE RESTAURANT

399. Möchten Sie etwas trinken?
Would you like something to drink?

400. Ja, bitte bringen Sie uns einen Wermut und ein Bier.
Yes, please bring us a vermouth and a beer.

401. Dürfte ich jetzt Ihre weitere Bestellungen entgegennehmen?
May I take the rest of your order now?

402. Was würden Sie empfehlen? Was ist Ihre Spezialität?
What would you recommend? What is the specialty of the house?

403. Der Kalbsbraten ist heute besonders gut. Die Forelle ist auch sehr zu empfehlen.
The veal roast is especially good today. I can also highly recommend the trout.

404. Gut, bringen Sie uns eine Portion Kalbsbraten und einmal Rehrücken.
All right, bring us one order of veal roast and one of saddle of venison.

405. Jawohl, mein Herr, und welche Beilagen wünschen die Herrschaften?

Yes, sir, and what side dishes would the lady and gentleman like with that?

406. Mit dem Kalbsbraten bringen Sie mir bitte Bratkartoffeln und Rosenkohl und mit dem Rehrücken, Rotkohl. Und mit dem Hauptgang möchten wir eine Flasche Moselwein.

Bring me home-fried potatoes and Brussels sprouts with the veal roast, and with the saddle of venison, red cabbage. And we would like a bottle of Moselle wine with our main course.

407. Welche Vorspeise und Suppe wünschen Sie?

Which appetizer and soup do you wish?

408. Russische Eier und Gänseleberpastete. Dann Erbsensuppe und einmal Fruchtsuppe.

Eggs à la Russe and pâté de foie gras. Then pea soup and one portion of fruit soup.

409. Möchten Sie auch Salat?

Would you also like some salad?

410. Ja, eine Portion gemischten Salat und einmal grünen Salat mit ein wenig Essig und Öl.

Yes, one mixed salad and one order of lettuce with a little oil and vinegar.

411. Als Nachspeise haben wir Eis, diverses Gebäck, Pflaumenkuchen und Obst.

For dessert we have: ice cream, assorted pastry, plum cake, and fruit.

412. Schön. Einmal Schokoladeneis und ein Stück Pflaumenkuchen. Eine Tasse Kaffee und eine Tasse Tee mit Sahne. Und Fräulein, bringen Sie uns noch einen Teelöffel. Dieser hier ist nicht ganz sauber.

Very well. One chocolate ice cream and one

piece of plum cake. One cup of coffee and
one cup of tea with cream. And waitress,
bring another spoon. This one is not quite
clean.

413. Bitte entschuldigen Sie.
Please excuse me.

**414. Können Sie mir bitte die Rechnung
bringen? Wir möchten ins Theater
und es ist höchste Zeit.**
Can you please bring the bill? We want to
go to the theatre and it is getting late.

415. Jawohl, mein Herr.
Yes, sir.

CHURCH

**416. Is there an English-speaking [priest, rabbi]
minister?**
Gibt es einen englisch-sprechenden [Priester,
Rabbiner] Geistlichen?
*gipt es Ī-nen ENG-lish SHPRESH-en-den [PREE-
ster, rah-BEE-ner] GĪST-lih-shen?*

417. A [Catholic] Protestant Church.
Eine [katholische] protestantische Kirche.
*Ī-nuh [kah-TOH-lih-shuh] pro-tes-TAHN-tih-shuh
KEER-shuh.*

418. An Anglican church.
Eine anglikanische Kirche.
Ī-nuh ahng-lih-KAH-nih-shuh KEER-shuh.

419. A synagogue.
Eine Synagoge.
Ī-nuh zew-nah-GO-guh.

420. When is [the service] the mass?
Wann ist [der Gottesdienst] die Messe?
vahn ist [dehr GAWT-tes-deenst] dee MES-suh?

SIGHTSEEING

421. I want a licensed guide who speaks English.
Ich möchte einen offiziellen, englisch-sprechenden
Reiseführer.
ish MERSH-tuh Ī-nen awf-fits-YEL-len, ENG-lish-shpreh-shen-den RĪ-zuh-few-rer.

422. What is the charge [per hour] per day?
Was sind die Gebühren [pro Stunde] pro Tag?
vahs zint dee geh-BEW-ren [pro SHTOON-duh] pro tahk?

423. I am interested [in architecture].
Ich interessiere mich [für Architektur].
ish in-teh-reh-SEE-ruh mish [fewr ahr-shih-tek-TOOR].

424. —— in painting.
für Malerei.
fewr mah-leh-RĪ.

425. —— in sculpture.
für Bildhauerei.
fewr BILT-how-er-RĪ.

426. Show us [the castle].
Zeigen Sie uns [das Schloss].
TSĪ-gen zee oons [dahs shlaws].

427. —— the cathedral.
den Dom.
dayn dohm.

428. —— the museums.
die Museen.
dee moo-ZAY-en.

429. When does it [open] close?
Wann wird [geöffnet] geschlossen?
vahn veert [geh-ERF-net] geh-SHLAWS-sen?

430. Where is the [entrance] exit?
Wo ist der [Eingang] Ausgang?
vo ist dehr [ĪN-gahng] OWS-gahng?

AMUSEMENTS

431. I should like to go [to a concert].
Ich möchte [in ein Konzert] gehen.
ish MERSH-tuh [in īn kawn-TSEHRT] GAY-en.

432. —— **to a matinee.**
zu einer Matinee.
tsoo Ī-ner mah-tee-NAY.

433. —— **to the movies.**
ins Kino.
ins KEE-no.

434. —— **to a night club.**
in ein Nachtlokal.
in īn NAHKHT-lo-kahl.

435. —— **to the opera.**
in die Oper.
in dee O-per.

436. —— **to the theatre.**
ins Theater.
ins tay-AH-ter.

437. —— **to the box office.**
zur Theaterkasse.
tsoor tay-AH-ter-kahs-suh.

438. What is playing tonight?
Was wird heute abend gegeben?
vahs veert HOY-tuh AH-bent geh-GAY-ben?

439. Is there an evening performance on holidays?
Findet eine Abendvorstellung an Feiertagen statt?
FIN-det Ī-nuh AH-bent-for-shtel-lŏong ahn FĪ-er-tah-gen shtaht?

440. Have you [any seats] for tonight?
Haben Sie [noch Plätze] für heute Abend?
HAH-ben zee [nawkh PLET-suh] fewr HOY-tuh AH-bent?

441. —— **an orchestra seat.**
einen Parkettplatz.
Ī-nen pahr-KET-plahts.

442. —— **a box.**
eine Loge.
Ī-nuh LO-zhuh.

443. In the balcony.
Im Balkon.
im bahl-KOHN.

444. Can I see well from there?
Kann ich dort gut sehen?
kahn ish dort goot ZAY-en?

445. Where can we go to dance?
Wo können wir tanzen?
vo KERN-nen veer TAHN-tsen?

446. May I have this dance?
Darf ich um diesen Tanz bitten?
dahrf ish ŏom DEE-zen tahnts BIT-ten?

SPORTS

447. Let's go [to the beach].
Lasst uns [zum Strand] gehen.
lahst oons [tsoom shtrahnt] GAY-en.

448. —— to the horse races.
zum Pferderennen.
tsoom PFEHR-duh-ren-nen.

449. —— to the swimming pool.
zum Schwimmbad.
tsoom SHVIM-baht.

450. I'd like to play [golf] tennis.
Ich möchte [Golf] Tennis spielen.
ish MERSH-tuh ["golf"] TEN-nis SHPEE-len.

451. Can we go [fishing]?
Können wir [angeln]?
KERN-nen veer [AHNG-eln]?

452. —— horseback riding.
reiten.
RĪ-ten.

453. —— skating.
schlittschuhlaufen.
SHLIT-shoo-low-fen.

454. —— skiing.
skilaufen.
SHEE-low-fen.

455. —— swimming.
schwimmen.
SHVIM-men.

BANK AND MONEY

456. Where is the nearest bank?
Wo ist die nächste Bank?
vo ist dee NAYK-stuh bahnk?

457. At which window can I cash this?
An welchem Schalter kann ich dies einlösen?
ahn VEL-shem SHAHL-ter kahn ish dees ĪN-ler-zen?

458. Will you cash [this personal check]?
Würden Sie bitte [diesen Scheck auf mein Privat-
konto] einlösen?
*VEWR-den zee BIT-tuh [DEE-zen shek owf min
pree-VAHT-kawn-toh] ĪN-ler-zen?*

459. —— a traveler's check?

einen Reisescheck.

I-nen RĪ-zuh-shek.

460. What is the exchange rate on the dollar?

Wie steht der Dollar im Kurs?

vee shtayt dehr DAWL-lahr im koors?

461. Can you change this for me?

Können Sie mir das wechseln?

KERN-nen zee meer dahs VEK-seln?

462. May I have fifty dollars' worth of German money?

Ich möchte fünfzig Dollar in deutsches Geld umwechseln.

ish MERSH-tuh FEWNF-tsish DAWL-lahr in DOYT-shes gelt OOM-vek-seln.

463. (Do not) give me many large bills.

Geben Sie mir (nicht) viele grosse Noten.

GAY-ben zee meer (nisht) FEE-luh GRO-suh NO-ten.

464. Can I have some small change?

Kann ich etwas Kleingeld haben?

kahn ish ET-vahs KLIN-gelt HAH-ben?

SHOPPING

465. I want to go shopping.

Ich möchte einkaufen gehen.

ish MERSH-tuh IN-kow-fen GAY-en.

466. I (do not) like this one.

Dies gefällt mir (nicht).

dees geh-FELT meer (nisht).

467. How much is it?

Wieviel kostet es?

VEE-feel KAW-stet es?

468. I prefer something [better].

Ich möchte lieber etwas [Besseres] haben.

ish MERSH-tuh LEE-ber ET-vahs [BES-ser-es] HAH-ben.

469. —— **cheaper.**
Billigeres.
BIL-lih-geh-res.

470. —— **smaller.**
Kleineres.
KLĪ-neh-res.

471. —— **larger.**
Grösseres.
GRĒR-seh-res.

472. Show me some others.
Zeigen Sie mir ein paar andere.
TSĪ-gen zee meer īn pahr AHN-deh-ruh.

473. May I try this on?
Darf ich dies anprobieren?
dahrf ish dees AHN-pro-bee-ren?

474. Can I order size 32?
Kann ich Grösse zweiunddreissig bestellen?
*kahn ish GRĒRS-suh TSVĪ-oont-DRĪ-sish beh-
SHTEL-len?*

475. Please take the measurements.
Bitte nehmen Sie Mass.
BIT-tuh NAY-men zee mahs.

476. Please measure [the length].
Bitte messen Sie [die Länge].
BIT-tuh MES-sen zee [dee LENG-uh].

477. —— **the width.**
die Breite.
dee BRĪ-tuh.

478. How long will it take?
Wie lange wird es dauern?
vee LAHNG-uh veert es DOW-ern?

479. I'll return later.
Ich werde später wiederkommen.
ish VEHR-duh SHPAY-ter VEE-der-kawm-men.

480. Can you ship it to New York City?
Können Sie es nach Neu York senden?
KĒR-nen zee es nahkh noy york ZEN-den?

481. Do I pay [the salesman]?
Soll ich [bei dem Verkäufer] bezahlen?
zawl ish [bī daym fer-KOY-fer] beh-TSAH-len?

482. —— **the salesgirl.**
bei der Verkäuferin.
bī dehr fer-KOY-feh-rin.

483. —— **the cashier.**
an der Kasse.
ahn dehr KAHS-suh.

484. Please send me a bill.
Bitte, schicken Sie mir eine Rechnung.
BIT-tuh, SHIK-ken zee meer Ī-nuh RESH-noong.

CLOTHING

485. I want to buy [a bathing cap].
Ich möchte [eine Bademütze] kaufen.
ish MERSH-tuh [Ī-nuh BAH-duh-mewt-tsuh] KOW- fen.

486. —— **a bathing suit.**
einen Badeanzug.
Ī-nen BAH-duh-ahn-tsook.

487. —— **a blouse.**
eine Bluse.
Ī-nuh BLOO-zuh.

488. —— **a brassiere.**
einen Büstenhalter.
Ī-nen BEW-sten-hahl-ter.

489. —— **an overcoat.**
einen Wintermantel.
Ī-nen VIN-ter-mahn-tel.

490. —— **a dress.**
ein Kleid.
in klīt.

491. —— **some children's dresses.**
Kinderkleider.
KIN-der-klī-der.

492. —— **a pair of gloves.**
ein Paar Handschuhe.
in pahr HAHNT-shoo-uh.

493. —— **a handbag.**
eine Damentasche.
Ī-nuh DAH-men-tah-shuh.

494. —— **one dozen handkerchiefs.**
ein Dutzend Taschentücher.
in DŎŎ-tsend TAH-shen-tew-sher.

495. —— **a hat.**
einen Hut.
Ī-nen hoot.

496. —— **a jacket.**
eine Jacke.
Ī-nuh YAHK-kuh.

497. —— some lingerie.
etwas Damenwäsche.
ET-vahs DAH-men-veh-shuh.

498. —— a nightgown.
ein Nachthemd.
īn NAHKHT-hemt.

499. —— a raincoat.
einen Regenmantel.
Ī-nen RAY-gen-mahn-tel.

500. —— a pair of shoes.
ein Paar Schuhe.
īn pahr SHOO-uh.

501. —— some shoelaces.
Schnürsenkel.
SHNEWR-zen-kel.

502. —— a skirt.
einen Rock.
Ī-nen rawk.

503. —— a pair of slippers.
ein Paar Pantoffeln.
īn pahr pahn-TAWF-feln.

504. —— a pair of socks.
ein Paar Socken.
īn pahr ZAWK-en.

505. —— a pair of nylon stockings.
ein Paar Perlon Strümpfe.
īn pahr PEHR-lawn SHTREWMP-fuh.

506. —— a shirt.
ein Hemd.
īn hemt.

507. —— a man's suit.
einen Herrenanzug.
Ī-nen HEHR-ren-ahn-tsŏok.

508. —— a sweater.
einen Pullover.
Ī-nen PŎOL-o-ver.

509. —— some neckties.
einige Krawatten.
Ī-nih-guh krah-VAHT-ten.

510. —— a pair of trousers.
ein Paar Hosen.
īn pahr HO-zen.

511. —— underwear.
Unterwäsche.
ŎON-ter-veh-shuh.

SUNDRIES

512. Do you have [some ashtrays]?
Haben Sie [Aschenbecher]?
HAH-ben zee [AH-shen-beh-sher]?

513. —— artists' supplies.
Zeichenmaterialien.
TSĪ-shen-mah-teh-ree-AHL-yen.

514. —— **a box of candy.**
eine Schachtel Süssigkeiten.
Ī-nuh SHAHKH-tel ƵEWS-sish-ki-ten.

515. —— **some china.**
etwas Geschirr.
ET-vahs geh-SHEER.

516. —— **a silver compact.**
eine silberne Puderdose.
Ī-nuh ƵIL-ber-nuh POO-der-doh-zuh.

517. —— **gold cuff links.**
goldene Manschettenknöpfe.
GAWL-deh-nuh mahn-SHET-ten-knerp-fuh.

518. —— **dolls.**
Puppen.
POOP-pen.

519. —— **earrings.**
Ohrringe.
AWR-ring-uh.

520. —— **musical instruments.**
Musikinstrumente.
moo-ƵEEK-in-shtroo-MEN-tuh.

521. —— **perfume.**
Parfüm.
pahr-FUN.

522. —— **pictures.**
Bilder.
BIL-der.

523. —— **a radio.**
ein Radio.
īn RAH-dee-o.

524. —— **records.**
Schallplatten.
SHAHL-plaht-ten.

525. —— **silverware.**
Silbersachen.
ƵIL-ber-sah-khen.

526. —— **some souvenirs.**
ein paar Andenken.
īn pahr AHN-denk-en.

527. —— **toys.**
Spielsachen.
SHPEEL-zah-khen.

528. —— **a silk umbrella.**
einen seidenen Regenschirm.
Ī-nen ƵĪ-deh-nen RAY-gen-sheerm.

529. —— **a wristwatch.**
eine Armbanduhr.
Ī-nuh AHRM-bahnt-oor.

COLORS

530. I want [a lighter shade].
Ich möchte [eine hellere Schattierung] haben.
*ish MĒRSH-tuh [Ī-nuh HEL-leh-ruh shah-TEE-roong]
HAH-ben.*

531. —— **a darker shade.**
eine dunklere Schattierung.
Ī-nuh DŎŎNK-leh-ruh shah-TEE-roong.

532. Black. Schwarz. *shvahrts.*

533. Blue. Blau. *blow.*

534. Brown. Braun. *brown.*

535. Gray. Grau. *grow.*

536. Green. Grün. *grewn.*

537. Orange. Orange. *aw-RAHN-zhuh.*

538. Pink. Rosa. *RO-zah.*

539. Purple. Lila. *LEE-lah.*

540. Red. Rot. *roht.*

541. White. Weiss. *vīs.*

542. Yellow. Gelb. *gelp.*

STORES

543. Where is [the bakery]?
Wo ist [die Bäckerei]?
vo ist [dee bek-eh-RĪ]?

544. —— **a candy store.**
ein Schokoladengeschäft.
īn shoh-koh-LAH-den-geh-sheft.

545. —— **a clothing store.**
ein Kleidergeschäft.
īn KLĪ-der-geh-sheft.

546. —— **a department store.**
ein Kaufhaus.
īn KOWF-hows.

547. —— a drugstore.
eine Drogerie.
Ī-nuh dro-geh-REE.

548. —— a pharmacy.
eine Apotheke.
Ī-nuh ah-paw-TAY-kuh.

549. —— a grocery.
ein Lebensmittelgeschäft.
īn LAY-bens-mit-tel-geh-sheft.

550. —— a hardware store.
ein Eisenwarengeschäft.
īn Ī-zen-vah-ren-geh-sheft.

551. —— a hat shop.
ein Hutladen.
īn HOOT-lah-den.

552. —— a jewelry store.
ein Juweliergeschäft.
īn yoo-veh-LEER-geh-sheft.

553. —— a market.
ein Markt.
īn mahrkt.

554. —— a meat market.
eine Fleischerei.
Ī-nuh flī-sheh-RĪ.

555. —— a pastry shop.
eine Konditorei.
Ī-nuh kawn-dih-taw-RĪ.

556. —— a shoemaker.
ein Schuhmacher.
īn SHOO-mah-kher.

557. —— a shoe store.
ein Schuhgeschäft.
īn SHOO-geh-sheft.

558. —— a tailor shop.
eine Schneiderei.
Ī-nuh shnī-deh-RĪ.

559. —— a watchmaker.
ein Uhrmacher.
īn OOR-mah-kher.

BOOKSTORE AND STATIONER'S

560. Where is there [a bookstore]?
Wo ist [ein Buchladen]?
vo ist [īn BOOKH-lah-den]?

561. —— a stationer.
ein Papiergeschäft.
īn pah-PEER-geh-sheft.

562. —— a news dealer.
ein Zeitungshändler.
īn TSĪ-toongs-hend-ler.

563. I want to buy [a book].
Ich möchte [ein Buch] kaufen.
ish MERSH-tuh [īn bookh] KOW-fen.

564. —— a guidebook.
ein Reisehandbuch.
ïn RĪ-zuh-hahnt-bookh.

565. —— a dictionary.
ein Wörterbuch.
ïn VĒRR-ter-bookh.

566. —— a magazine.
eine Zeitschrift.
Ī-nuh TSĪT-shrift.

567. —— a map of Germany.
eine Karte von Deutschland.
Ī-nuh KAHR-tuh fun DOYTSH-lahnt.

568. —— a newspaper.
eine Zeitung.
Ī-nuh TSĪ-toong.

569. I should like [some envelopes].
Ich möchte [Kuverts] kaufen.
ish MĒRSH-tuh [koo-VEHRS] KOW-fen.

570. —— writing paper.
Schreibpapier.
SHRĪP-pah-peer.

571. —— a pencil.
einen Bleistift.
Ī-nen BLĪ-shtift.

572. —— picture postcards.
Ansichtskarten.
AHN-zishts-kahr-ten.

573. —— wrapping paper.
Packpapier.
PAHK-pah-peer.

574. —— string.
Bindfaden.
BINT-fah-den.

CIGAR STORE

575. Where is the nearest cigar store?
Wo ist der nächste Zigarrenladen?
vo ist dehr NAYK-stuh tsih-GAHR-ren-lah-den?

576. I want [some cigars].
Ich möchte [ein paar Zigarren] haben.
ish MĒRSH-tuh [ïn pahr tsih-GAHR-ren] HAH-ben.

577. —— **a pack of American cigarettes.**
ein Päckchen amerikanische Zigaretten.
īn PEK-shen ah-may-ree-KAH-nish-uh tsih-gah- RET-ten.

578. —— **a leather cigarette case.**
ein echtledernes Zigarettenetui.
īn ESHT-lay-der-nes tsih-gah-RET-ten-AY- twee.

579. —— **a lighter.**
ein Feuerzeug.
īn FOY-er-tsoyk.

580. —— **pipe tobacco.**
Pfeifentabak.
PFĪ-fen-tah-bahk.

581. —— **Do you have a match?**
Haben Sie ein Streichholz?
HAH-ben zee īn SHTRĪKH-hohlts?

CAMERA SHOP

582. I want a roll of film for this camera.
Ich möchte einen Film für diesen Apparat haben.
ish MERSH-tuh Ī-nen film fewr DEE-zen ah-pah-
RAHT HAH-ben.

**583. What is the charge for developing a roll of
color film?**
Was kostet es einen Farbfilm zu entwickeln?
vahs KAW-stet es Ī-nen FAHRP-film tsoo ent-VIK-
keln?

584. When will they be ready?
Wann werden sie fertig sein?
vahn VEHR-den zee FEHR-tish zin?

585. May I take a snapshot of you?
Dürfte ich Sie fotographieren?
DEWRF-tuh ish zee fo-toh-grah-FEE-ren?

PHARMACY

**586. Where is there a pharmacy where English is
spoken?**
Gibt es hier eine Apotheke wo jemand Englisch
spricht?

gipt es heer *Ī-nuh ah-paw-TAY-kuh vo YAY-mahnt*
ENG-lish shprisht?

587. Can you fill this prescription immediately?
Können Sie dieses Rezept sofort zubereiten?
KĒR-nen zee DEE-zes ray-TSEPT zo-FORT
TSOO-beh-rī-ten?

588. Do you have [adhesive tape]?
Haben Sie [Heftpflaster]?
HAH-ben zee [HEFT-pflah-ster]?

589. —— antiseptic.
ein Desinfektionsmittel.
īn des-in-fek-TSYAWNS-mit-tel.

590. —— aspirin.
Aspirin.
ahs-pee-REEN.

591. —— a hairbrush.
eine Haarbürste.
Ī-nuh HAHR-bewr-stuh:

592. —— a toothbrush.
eine Zahnbürste.
Ī-nuh TSAHN-bewr-stuh.

593. —— a comb.
einen Kamm.
Ī-nen kahm.

594. —— a deodorant.
(ein) Geruchbefreiungsmittel.
(īn) geh-ROOKH-beh-frī-oongs-mit-tel.

595. —— a mild laxative.
ein mildes Abführmittel.
in MIL-des AHP-fewr-mit-tel.

596. —— a razor.
einen Rasierapparat.
Ī-nen rah-ZEER-ah-pah-raht.

597. —— razor blades.
Rasierklingen.
rah-ZEER-kling-en.

598. —— sanitary napkins.
Binden.
BIN-den.

599. —— a sedative.
ein Beruhigungsmittel.
īn beh-ROO-ih-goongs-mit-tel.

600. —— shampoo.
ein Shampoo.
īn SHAHM-poo.

601. —— shaving cream (brushless).
eine Rasierkreme (ohne Pinsel).
Ī-nuh rah-ZEER-kray-muh (O-nuh PIN-zel).

602. —— **a thermometer.**
ein Thermometer.
īn tehr-maw-MAY-ter.

603. —— **a tube of toothpaste.**
eine Tube Zahnpasta.
Ī-nuh TOO-buh TSAHN-pahs-tah.

LAUNDRY AND DRY CLEANING

604. Where is [the laundry]?
Wo ist [die Wäscherei]?
vo ist [dee veh-sheh-RĪ]?

605. —— **the dry cleaner.**
die chemische Reinigungsanstalt.
dee SHAY-mih-shuh RĪ-nih-goongs-ahn-shtahlt.

606. I want these shirts [washed] mended.
Ich möchte diese Hemden [waschen lassen]
flicken lassen.
*ish MERSH-tuh DEE-zuh HEM-den [VAH-shen
LAHS-sen] FLIK-ken LAHS-sen.*

607. No starch.
Nicht stärken.
nisht SHTEHR-ken.

608. I want this suit [cleaned] pressed.
Ich möchte diesen Anzug [reinigen lassen]
bügeln lassen.
*ish MERSH-tuh DEE-zen AHN-tsook [RĪ-nih-gen
LAHS-sen] BEW-geln LAHS-sen.*

609. The belt is missing.
Der Gürtel fehlt.
dehr GEWR-tel faylt.

610. Can you sew on this button?
Können Sie diesen Knopf annähen?
KERN-nen zee DEE-zen knawpf AHN-nay-en?

611. Repair the zipper.
Reparieren Sie den Reissverschluss.
reh-pah-REE-ren zee dayn RĪS-fehr-shlōōs.

BARBERSHOP AND BEAUTY PARLOR

612. Where is there [a beauty parlor]?
Wo ist [ein Damen-Friseur]?
vo ist [īn DAH-men-free-zẽrr]?

613. —— a barber shop.
ein Herren-Friseur.
īn HEHR-ren-free-zẽrr.

614. A haircut, please.
Haarschneiden, bitte.
HAHR-shnī-den, BIT-tuh.

615. No lotion, please.
Kein Haarwasser, bitte.
kīn HAHR-vahs-ser, BIT-tuh.

616. Please give me a shave.
Bitte rasieren Sie mich.
BIT-tuh rah-ZEE-ren zee mish.

617. Please give me a shampoo.
Bitte schampunieren Sie mich.
BIT-tuh shahm-poo-NEE-ren zee mish.

618. A hair set.
Eine Wasserwelle.
Ī-nuh VAHS-ser-vel-luh.

619. A permanent.
Eine Dauerwelle.
Ī-nuh DOW-er-vel-luh.

620. A manicure.
Eine Maniküre.
Ī-nuh mah-nee-KEW-ruh.

621. A facial.
Eine Gesichtsmassage.
Ī-nuh geh-ZISHTS-mah-sah-zhuh.

HEALTH AND ILLNESS

622. I wish to see an American doctor.
Ich möchte einen amerikanischen Arzt aufsuchen.
*ish MÊRSH-tuh Ī-nen ah-may-ree-KAH-nish-en ahrtst
OWF-zoo-khen.*

623. Is the doctor [at home] in his office?
Ist der Herr Doktor [zu Hause] in seinem
Sprechzimmer?
*ist dehr hehr DAWK-tor [tsoo HOW-zuh] in ZĪ-nem
SHPRESH-tsim-mer?*

624. I do not sleep well.
Ich schlafe nicht gut.
ish SHLAH-fuh nisht goot.

625. I have [a headache].
Ich habe [Kopfschmerzen].
ish HAH-buh [KAWPF-shmehr-tsen].

626. —— an allergy.
eine Allergie.
Ī-nuh ahl-lehr-GEE.

627. —— a cold.
eine Erkältung.
Ī-nuh ehr-KEL-toong.

628. —— a cough.
einen Husten.
Ī-nen HOO-sten.

629. —— constipation.
Verstopfung.
fehr-STAWP-foong.

630. —— diarrhea.
Durchfall.
DOORSH-fahl.

631. —— a fever.
Fieber.
FEE-ber.

632. —— a sore throat.
Halsschmerzen.
HAHLS-shmehr-tsen.

633. I have indigestion.
Ich habe mir den Magen verdorben.
ish HAH-buh meer dayn MAH-gen fehr-DOR-ben.

634. I am nauseated.
Mir ist übel.
meer ist EW-bel.

635. Must I stay in bed?
Muss ich im Bett bleiben?
moos ish im bet BLĪ-ben?

636. I feel [better] worse.
Ich fühle mich [besser] schlechter.
ish FEW-luh mish [BES-ser] SHLESH-ter.

637. There is something in my eye.
Mir ist etwas ins Auge geflogen.
meer ist ET-vahs ins OW-guh geh-FLOH-gen.

638. I have a pain in my chest.
Ich habe Brustschmerzen.
ish HAH-buh BROOST-shmehr-tsen.

639. When do you think I'll be able to continue my trip?
Wann, glauben Sie, kann ich meine Reise fortsetzen?
vahn, GLOW-ben zee, kahn ish MĪ-nuh RĪ-zuh FAWRT-zet-tsen?

DENTIST

640. Do you know a good dentist?
Kennen Sie einen guten Zahnarzt?
KEN-nen zee Ī-nen GOO-ten TSAHN-ahrtst?

641. This tooth hurts.
Dieser Zahn schmerzt.
DEE-zer tsahn shmehrtst.

642. Can you fix it temporarily?
Können Sie es provisorisch in Ordnung bringen?
KERN-nen zee es pro-vee-ZOH-rish in ORD-noong BRING-en?

643. I have lost a filling.
Ich habe eine Plombe verloren.
ish HAH-buh Ī-nuh PLOHM-buh fehr-LO-ren.

644. I do not want the tooth extracted.
Ich möchte mir den Zahn nicht ziehen lassen.
ish MERSH-tuh meer dayn tsahn nisht TSEE-en LAHS-sen.

CONVERSATION AT THE POST OFFICE

645. Ich möchte diesen Brief nach den Vereinigten Staaten schicken. Wieviel Porto kostet das?
I would like to send this letter to the United States. How much postage is that please?

646. Mit gewöhnlicher Post dreissig Pfennig, per Luftpost sechzig Pfennig.
By regular mail 30 Pfennig. By airmail 60 Pfennig.

647. Geben Sie mir bitte zwanzig Marken à 10 und fünf à 20.
Please let me have twenty 10-Pfennig stamps and five 20-Pfennig stamps.

648. Das macht insgesamt drei Mark. Der Briefkasten ist gleich hier links.
That will be three Marks altogether. The mailbox is right here to the left.

649. Vielen Dank. Wo kann ich ein Paket aufgeben?
Thank you very much. Where can I mail a package?

650. Bei der Paketannahme. Nächster Schalter rechts.
At the parcel-post window. Next window to the right.

651. Was enthält Ihr Paket?
What does your parcel contain?

652. Nur ein paar Bücher und Geschenke.
Only a few books and presents.

653. Ist irgend etwas Zerbrechliches darin?
Does it contain anything breakable?

654. Nein. Kann ich das Paket versichern? Wieviel würde das kosten?
No. Can I insure the package? How much would that be?

655. Wie hoch wollen Sie es denn versichern? Es kostet fünfzig Pfennig pro fünfundzwanzig Mark Versicherung.
For how much do you want to insure it? The rate is 50 Pfennig per 25 Mark insurance.

**656. Gut, bitte versichern Sie es für fünfundsieb-
zig Mark.**
Very well, please insure it for 75 Marks.

**657. Bitte füllen Sie dieses Formular aus. Das
macht zusammen vier Mark neunund-
vierzig Pfennig; zwei neunundneunzig
Porto und eine Mark fünfzig für die
Versicherung.**
Please fill out this form. The total charge is
4 Marks 49; 2 Marks 99 for the postage and
1 Mark 50 for the insurance.

658. Bekomme ich einen Empfangsschein?
Do I get a receipt?

**659. Jawohl. Bitte unterschreiben Sie dieses
Formular.**
Yes. Please sign this form.

660. Gut. Recht vielen Dank.
Very well. Thank you very much.

AT THE TELEPHONE

661. Zentrale? Fernamt bitte.
Operator? Long distance, please.

662. Einen Augenblick, bitte.
One moment, please.

**663. Fernamt? Ich möchte ein Ferngespräch
nach Mannheim anmelden. Bitte ver-
binden Sie mich mit Mannheim sechs null
vier zwo* sieben.**
Long distance? I would like to place a long-
distance call to Mannheim. Please connect
me with Mannheim 6-0427.

664. Mit Voranmeldung?
Person-to-person call?

665. Nein.
No.

---

*In telephoning, 2 is called "zwo" (tsvo) instead of "zwei" to avoid confusion with "drei" (three).

666. Ihre Nummer, bitte?
Your number, please?

667. Bremerhaven neun sieben fünf acht. Und bitte unterbrechen Sie mich nach drei Minuten.
Bremerhaven 9758. And please let me know when three minutes are up.

668. Wie Sie wünschen. Ihr Teilnehmer meldet sich schon.
As you wish. Your party is answering already.

669. Hallo; hier Heinz Mahler. Könnte ich mit Herrn Gustav Leander sprechen?
Hello. This is Heinz Mahler speaking. May I speak to Mr. Gustav Leander?

670. Wie, bitte? Sprechen Sie etwas lauter bitte. Die Verbindung ist nicht besonders gut.
I beg your pardon; speak a bit louder, please. The connection is not very good.

671. Hier Heinz Mahler. Ich möchte Herrn Leander sprechen.
This is Heinz Mahler. I'd like to speak to Mr. Leander.

672. Ach so. Ja, aber Herr Leander ist leider nicht zu Hause and wird voraussichtlich nicht vor halb zehn heute Abend nach Hause kommen.
Oh, I see. But Mr. Leander is unfortunately not at home and will probably not return until 9:30 this evening.

673. Hallo, hallo, Fernamt, Sie haben uns unterbrochen!
Hello, hello, long distance, you have cut us off!

674. Verzeihung. Ich stelle den Anschluss gleich wieder her.
I am sorry; I'll connect you again right away.

675. Hallo, Mannheim? Könnten Sie etwas an Herrn Leander ausrichten? Sagen Sie ihm bitte, dass Heinz Mahler angerufen hat. Ich werde Sonntag in Mannheim ankommen und im Schweizer Hof übernachten und zwar in Zimmer sechshundertvier.

Hello, Mannheim? Could you leave a message for Mr. Leander? Please tell him that Heinz Mahler called. I am arriving in Mannheim on Sunday and will spend the night at the Hotel Switzerland. My room number will be 604.

676. Einen Augenblick, bitte. Ich möchte mir das aufschreiben. Schweizer Hof. Haben Sie Zimmer fünfhundertvier gesagt?

One moment, please. I'd like to write that down. Hotel Switzerland. Did you say Room 504?

677. Nein, Sie haben mich falsch verstanden; sechshundertvier.

No, you misunderstood me; 604.

678. Schön, alles in Ordnung.

Very good.

679. Verzeihen Sie die Störung.

I'm sorry to have bothered you.

680. Nicht im Geringsten. Ich werde Herrn Leander alles bestens ausrichten.

Not at all. I'll see to it that Mr. Leander gets the message.

681. Vielen Dank Auf Wiedersehen.

Thanks very much. Goodbye.

682. Auf Wiedersehen.

Goodbye.

SENDING A CABLEGRAM

683. Ich möchte ein Telegramm nach den Vereinigten Staaten aufgeben. Wie hoch ist die Gebühr?

I should like to send a cablegram to the United States. What is the rate?

684. Ein gewöhnliches Telegramm kostet pro Wort dreiundneunzig Pfennig nach Neu York und eine Mark neunundzwanzig ausserhalb Neu York.

A regular telegram is 93 Pfennigs per word to New York City and 1 Mark 29 outside New York.

685. Was ist die Mindestgebühr?

What is the minimum?

686. Die Mindestgebühr beträgt nur eine Mark fünfzig.

The minimum is only 1 Mark 50.

687. Könnte ich stattdessen ein Brieftelegramm nach Amerika senden?

Could I send a night letter instead to America?

688. Jawohl, Sie können ein Brieftelegramm zu ermässigter Gebühr senden. Allerdings ist die Mindestgebühr zehn Mark dreiundzwanzig nach Neu York. Dafür können Sie zweiundzwanzig Worte schreiben.

Yes, you can send a night letter at a lower rate. In that case, the minimum is 10 Marks 23 to New York, for which you are allowed 22 words.

689. Wann würde das Brieftelegramm ankommen?

When would the night letter arrive?

690. Nicht vor morgen früh.

Not before tomorrow morning.

691. Und das gewöhnliche Telegramm?

And the regular telegram?

692. Voraussichtlich binnen fünf Stunden.

Most probably within five hours.

693. Dann werde ich ein gewöhnliches Telegramm aufgeben. Könnte ich ein paar Formulare haben?

In that case I'll send a regular telegram. Could I have a couple of forms?

694. Sie liegen dort auf dem Schreibpult. Schreiben Sie bitte Ihren Namen und Ihre Adresse in Blockschrift und bringen Sie mir das ausgefüllte Formular.

There are some on the desk over there. Please print your name and address and return the filled-in form to me.

695. Vielen Dank.

Thanks very much.

TIME

696. What time is it?
Wieviel Uhr ist es?
VEE-feel oor ist es?

697. It is early.
Es ist früh.
es ist frew.

698. It is (too) late.
Es ist (zu) spät.
es ist (tsoo) shpayt.

699. It is two o'clock A.M. (P.M.).
Es ist zwei Uhr (vierzehn Uhr).*
es ist tsvī oor. (FEER-tsayn oor).

700. It is half-past three.
Es ist halb vier.
es ist hahlp feer.

701. It is a quarter past four.
Es ist ein Viertel nach vier.
es ist īn FEER-tel nahkh feer.

702. It is a quarter to five.
Es ist ein Viertel vor fünf.
es ist īn FEER-tel for fewnf.

703. At ten minutes to six.
Um zehn Minuten vor sechs.
oom tsayn min-OO-ten for zeks.

704. At twenty minutes past seven.
Um zwanzig Minuten nach sieben.
oom TSVAHN-tsish min-OO-ten nahkh ZEE-ben.

---

*The twenty-four-hour system is more commonly used in Europe than in the United States. One to twelve P.M. are therefore expressed in numbers from thirteen to twenty-four.

705. Day. Tag. *tahk.*   **706. Night.** Nacht. *nahkht.*

707. Midnight. Mitternacht. *MIT-ter-nahkht.*

708. Today. Heute. *HOY-tuh.*

709. Tomorrow. Morgen. *MOR-gen.*

710. In the morning. Morgens. *MOR-gens.*

711. In the afternoon. Nachmittags.
NAHKH-mit-tahks.

712. In the evening. Abends. *AH-bents.*

713. Yesterday. Gestern. *GES-tern.*

714. Last night. Gestern Abend. *GES-tern AH-bent.*

715. Last month. Voriger Monat.
FOR-ih-ger mo-NAHT.

716. Last year. Voriges Jahr. *FOR-ih-ges yahr.*

717. Next week. Nächste Woche.
NAYK-stuh VAW-khuh.

DAYS OF THE WEEK

718. Monday. Montag. *MOHN-tahk.*

719. Tuesday. Dienstag. *DEENS-tahk.*

720. Wednesday. Mittwoch. *MIT-vawkh.*

721. Thursday. Donnerstag. *DAWN-ners-tahk.*

722. Friday. Freitag. *FRĪ-tahk.*

723. Saturday. Samstag oder Sonnabend.*
ZAHMS-tahk O-der ZAWN-ah-bent.

724. Sunday. Sonntag. *ZAWN-tahk.*

MONTHS

725. January. Januar. *YAH-noo-ahr.*

726. February. Februar. *FAY-broo-ahr.*

727. March. März. *mehrts.*

728. April. April. *ah-PRIL.*

729. May. Mai. *mī.*

730. June. Juni. *YOO-nee.*

731. July. Juli. *YOO-lee.*

732. August. August. *ow-GŎOST.*

733. September. September. *zep-TEM-ber.*

734. October. Oktober. *awk-TOH-ber.*

735. November. November. *no-VEM-ber.*

736. December. Dezember. *day-TSEM-ber.*

SEASONS AND WEATHER

737. Spring. Frühling. *FREW-ling.*

738. Summer. Sommer. *ZAWM-mer.*

739. Autumn. Herbst. *hehrpst.*

740. Winter. Winter. *VIN-ter.*

741. It is warm. Es ist warm. *es ist vahrm.*

742. It is cold. Es ist kalt. *es ist kahlt.*

743. The weather is good. Das Wetter ist schön.
dahs VET-ter ist shern.

---

* Both forms are in common use.

744. The weather is bad. Das Wetter ist schlecht.
dahs VET-ter ist shlesht.

745. It is raining. Es regnet. *es RAYG-net.*

NUMBERS

746. One. Eins. *īns.*   **Two.** Zwei. *tsvī.*

Three. Drei. *drī.*   **Four.** Vier. *feer.*

Five. Fünf. *fewnf.*   **Six.** Sechs. *zeks.*

Seven. Sieben. *ZEE-ben.*   **Eight.** Acht. *ahkht.*

Nine. Neun. *noyn.*   **Ten.** Zehn. *tsayn.*

Eleven. Elf. *elf.*   **Twelve.** Zwölf. *tsverlf.*

Thirteen. Dreizehn. *DRĪ-tsayn.*

Fourteen. Vierzehn. *FIHR-tsayn.*

Fifteen. Fünfzehn. *FEWNF-tsayn.*

Sixteen. Sechzehn. *ZESH-tsayn.*

Seventeen. Siebzehn. *ZEEP-tsayn.*

Eighteen. Achtzehn. *AHKHT-tsayn.*

Nineteen. Neunzehn. *NOYN-tsayn.*

Twenty. Zwanzig. *TSVAHN-tsish.*

Twenty-one. Einundzwanzig.   **Twenty-two.** Zweiundzwanzig.
ĪN-oont-tsvahn-tsish.   *TSVĪ-oont-tsvahn-tsish.*

Thirty. Dreissig. *DRĪ-sish.*   **Forty.** Vierzig. *FIHR-tsish.*

Fifty. Fünfzig. *FEWNF-tsish.*   **Sixty.** Sechzig. *ZESH-tsish.*

Seventy. Siebzig. *ZEEP-tsish.*

Eighty. Achtzig. *AHKHT-tsish.*

Ninety. Neunzig. *NOYN-tsish.*

One hundred. Einhundert. *ĪN-hoon-dert.*

Two hundred. Zweihundert. *TSVĪ-hoon-dert.*

One thousand. Eintausend. *ĪN-tow-zent.*

Two thousand. Zweitausend. *TSVĪ-tow-zent.*

One million. Eine Million. *Ī-nuh meel-YOHN.*

INDEX

The sentences, words and phrases in this book are numbered consecutively from 1 to 746. All entries in this book refer to these numbers. In addition, each major section heading (CAPITALIZED) is indexed according to page number (**boldface**). Parts of speech are indicated by the following italic abbreviations: *adj.* for adjective, *adv.* for adverb, *conj.* for conjunction, *n.* for noun, *prep.* for preposition, *pro.* for pronoun and *v.* for verb. Parentheses are used for explanations.

Because of the large volume of material indexed, cross-indexing has generally been avoided. Phrases or groups of words will usually be found under only one of their components, e.g., "bathing suit" appears only under "bathing," even though there is a separate entry for "suit" alone. If you do not find a phrase under one word, try another.

driver's license 196
drugstore 547
dry cleaner 605
duck 348
dutiable 107

Early 697
earrings 519
east 130
eat 296
egg 337–342
eight 746
eighteen 746
eighty 746
eleven 746
empty 206
engine 214
English (language) 44
English-speaking 416
enough 307
entrance 430
envelope 569
especially 403
evening: in the — 711;
  good — 2
everything 103
excellent 317
excess 171
exchange rate, what is the
  460
excuse me 62
exit 430
extract *v.* 644
eye 637

Facial *n.* 621
family 21
far 148
fat (rich food) 229
February 726
feel 636
fever 631
fifteen 746
fifty 746
fill (prescription) 587; —
  out 657
filling (dental) 643
film 582; color — 583
find 86
fine 17
finished 110
first 153
fish *n.* 349
fishing, go 451
five 746
fix 642
flight 169

food 317
FOOD LIST **p. 25**
for 233
forget 89
fork 291
form 657
forty 746
forward *adv.* 146; *v.* 262
four 746
fourteen 746
Frankfurt 159
free (= available) 191
Friday 722
fried 301
friend 14, 85
front: in — of 144
fruit 411; — juice 329;
  — soup 408
FRUITS **p. 28**
full 206
furnished 220

Garage 198
gas 226; — station 197
German *adj.* 462; (lan-
  guage) 47
Germany 567
get off 188
gift 106
girl 70
give 207
glass 265
gloves 492
go 116; (= lead) 201;
  let's — 447
gold 517
golf 450
good 1, 200, 217, 640;
  (weather) 743
goodbye 4
goose 350
grape 381
grapefruit 380
gravy 328
gray 535
green 536
grocery 549
guide 421
guidebook 564

Hairbrush 591
haircut 614
hair set 618
half-past 700
ham 342
Hamburg 151
handbag 87, 493

handkerchief 494
handle *v.* 115
hanger 250
happy: — birthday 29;
  — New Year 30
hard-boiled 339
hardware store 550
hat 495; — shop 551
have 101, 225
he 89
headache 625
headwaiter 282
health, to your 274
HEALTH AND
  ILLNESS **p. 47**
hello 3
help 84
her 87
here 97
his 89
holiday 439
horseback riding, go 452
horse races 448
hotel 217
HOTEL **p. 17**
hour 692; per — 192
how 77; — are you 16;
  — are things 18; —
  far 148; — long (time)
  478; — many 170; —
  much 467
hundred: one — 746; two
  — 746
hungry, I am 42
hurry, I am in a 43
hurt 641
husband 8

I 33
ice 319
identification papers 99
in 142
included 261
indigestion, have 633
inexpensive 218
instead 687
instrument, musical 520
insurance 657
insure 654
interested, I am 423
international 196
introduce 6
it is 697

Jacket 496
jam 334
January 725

jewelry store 552
juice: fruit — 329; orange
— 330; tomato — 331
July 805
June 804

Keep 316
key 90; room — 256
kilo 170
kilometer 192
knife 292
know (a fact) 51; (be ac-
quainted with) 640

Ladies' room 74
lamb 351
large 463
larger 471
last (= previous) 715, 716
late 698
later 245
laundry 604
LAUNDRY AND DRY
CLEANING p. 46
laxative 595
leather 578
leave 174, 259; (some-
thing) 114
left, to the 133
lemon 390
lemonade 391
length 476
letter 257, 645
lettergram 689
lettuce 367
licensed 421
light adj. 266
lighter adj. (color) 530;
n. 579
like 302; I — this 466;
I — you 27
lingerie 497
listen 82
liter 205
little, a 47, 245
liver 352
lobster 353
long distance 661
look: — for 85; — out 83
lose 87
lost-and-found desk 92
lotion (hair) 615
louder 670
lubricate 210
lunch 277

Magazine 566

mail n. 262; v. 649
mailbox 648
MAKING YOURSELF
UNDERSTOOD p. 4
man 71
manager 255
manicure 620
Mannheim 663
many 463
map 204
March 727
Mark (currency) 655
market 553; meat — 554
mass 420
match n. 581
matinee 432
matter, it doesn't 66
May 729
may I 6, 585
me 50
meal 232
mean v. 55
measure 476
measurements 475
meat 302
mechanic 199
medium (meat) 303
meet: glad to — you 15
melon 382
mend 606
men's room 73
menu 288
message 257
middle, in the 142
midnight 707
mild 595
milk 389
million, one 746
minimum (charge) 685
minister 416
minute 703
Miss 6
miss v. 215
missing 609
mistake 314
misunderstand 677
mixed 410
moment 81
Monday 718
money 89
month 715
MONTHS p. 57
monument 144
more 306
morning: good — 1; in
the — 710
motor 215

movies 433
Mr. 6
Mrs. 6
Munich 121
museum 428
mushroom 368
must 103
mustard 327
my 280, 281

Name: my — is 32
napkin 290
nauseated, I am 634
near 186
nearest 575
necktie 509
news dealer 562
newspaper 568
New York City 480
next 203
night 706; — club 434;
— letter 687
nightgown 498
nine 746
nine-fifteen 242
nineteen 746
ninety 746
no 59
north 128
not 680
nothing 101
November 735
now 401
number 666
NUMBERS p. 58
nylon 505

Oatmeal 333
o'clock (= hour) 699
October 734
office 623
oil (food) 325; (lubricat-
ing) 208
omelet 336
one 746
onion 369
only 46
open v. 103; when does
it — 429
opera 435
operator (telephone) 661
orange (color) 537; (fruit)
483
order n. 401; v. 309, 474
other 139
outside prep. 684
overcoat 489